All the
Best
Songs
of Praise &
Worship
4

More Contemporary Favorites

lillenas
PUBLISHING COMPANY

Copyright © 2011 by Lillenas Publishing Company, Box 419527,
Kansas City, MO 64141. All rights reserved. Litho in U.S.A.

www.lillenas.com

1 Our God*

Exod. 15:11; Matt. 11:5; John 2:1-11; Rom. 8:31

J. R., C. T., M. R. and J. M.

JESSE REEVES, CHRIS TOMLIN,
MATT REDMAN and JONAS MYRIN

1. Wa - ter You turned in - to wine,
2, 3. In - to the dark - ness You shine,

o - pened the eyes of the blind; There's no one
out of the ash - es we rise; There's no one

like You, none like You.
like You, none like You.

Our God is great - er,

*This song is included on the companion recording. Intro on recording is 8 measures.

© 2003 and this arr. © 2008 Integrity's Hosanna! Music/ASCAP (adm. at EMICMGPublishing.com).
All rights reserved. International copyright secured. Used by permission.

Hosanna*

Ps. 24:7-10; Mark 11:9-10; 13:26

B. F. ♩ = ca. 74

BROOKE FRASER

1. I see the King of Glo - ry com - ing on the clouds with fire;
2. I see a gen - er - a - tion ris - ing up to take their place

The whole earth shakes, the whole earth shakes.
With self - less faith, with self - less faith.

I see His love and mer - cy
I see a near re - viv - al

wash - ing o - ver all our sin; The peo - ple sing,
stir - ring as we pray and seek; We're on our knees,

*This song is included on the companion recording. Intro on recording is 8 measures.

Copyright © 2007 Hillsong Publishing (APRA) (adm. in the US and Canada
at EMICMGPublishing.com) All rights reserved. Used by permission.

3

Happy Day*

Matt. 28:1-10; Rev. 7:15-17

T. H. and B. C.

TIM HUGHES and
BEN CANTELON

1. The great-est day in his - to - ry,
2. When I stand in that place,

Death is beat-en, You have res - cued me; Sing it out,
Free at last, meet - ing face to face; I am Yours,

Je - sus is a - live.
Je - sus, You are mine.

The emp-ty cross, the emp - ty grave,
End - less joy, per - fect peace,

*This song is included on the companion recording. Intro on recording is 8 measures.

Copyright © 2006 Thankyou Music (PRS) (adm. worldwide at EMICMGPublishing.com excluding Europe which is adm. by Kingswaysongs). All rights reserved. Used by permission.

4 I Will Rise*

Ps. 73:26; 1 Thess. 4:16-18; Rev. 5:12-14; 17:14

L. G., J. R., M. M. and C. T.

LOUIE GIGLIO, JESSE REEVES,
MATT MAHER and CHRIS TOMLIN

*This song is included on the companion recording. Intro on recording is 8 measures.

Copyright © 2008 Thankyou Music (PRS) (adm. worldwide at EMICMGPublishing.com
excluding Europe which is adm. by Kingswaysongs)/worshiptogether.com Songs (ASCAP)/
sixsteps Music (ASCAP)/Spiritandsong.Com Pub (BMI)/Vamos Publishing (ASCAP)
(adm. at EMICMGPublishing.com). All rights reserved. Used by permission.

He Reigns*

Rev. 19:6-7

STEVE TAYLOR
and PETER FURLER

S. T. and P. F.

1. It's the song of the re-deemed ris-ing from the Af - ri - can plain.

It's the song of the for-giv - en drown-ing out the Am - a - zon rain; The song of A - sian be-liev - ers filled with God's ho - ly fire.

*This song is included on the companion recording. Intro on recording is 8 measures.

Copyright © 2003 Ariose Music (ASCAP) (adm. at EMICMGPublishing.com)/
Soylent Tunes (SESAC). All rights reserved. Used by permission.

6

My Savior Lives*

Ps. 73:26; 1 Thess. 4:16-18; Rev. 5:12-14; 17:14

G. P. and J. E.

♩ = ca. 134

VERSE

GLENN PACKIAM
and JON EGAN

1. Our God will reign for - ev - er and all the world will know His name; Ev - 'ry - one to - geth - er sing the song of the re - deemed.

2. The King has come from heav - en and dark - ness trem - bles at His name; "Vic - to - ry for - ev - er!" is the song of the re - deemed.

CHORUS

I know that my

*This song is included on the companion recording. Intro on recording is 8 measures.

© 2006 Vertical Worship Songs (ASCAP) (adm. at EMICMGPublishing.com).
All rights reserved. Used by permission.

Stronger*

Luke 19:10; Rev. 17:14

R. M. and B. F.

REUBEN MORGAN
and BEN FIELDING

1. There is love that came for us,
(2. Faith - ful) - ness none can de - ny;

Hum - bled
Through the

to a sin - ner's cross.
storm and thro' the fire.

You broke my shame and sin - ful -
There is truth that sets me

ness;
free;

You rose a - gain,
Je - sus Christ,

vic - to - ri - ous!
who lives in

me!

2. Faith - ful

You are

*This song is included on the companion recording. Intro on recording is 11 measures.

Copyright © 2007 Hillsong Publishing (APRA) (adm. in the US and Canada
at EMICMGPublishing.com) All rights reserved. Used by permission.

8

At the Cross*

Ps. 139:1-3; John 15:13; Rom. 8:35-39

D. Z. and R. M.

DARLENE ZSCHECH
and REUBEN MORGAN

1st time: Unison
2nd time: 2-part

1. O Lord, You've searched me,
2. Your ho - ly pres - ence,

You know my way;
sur - round - ing me;

E - ven when I fail
In ev - 'ry sea -

You, I know You love me.
- son I know You love me,

I know You love me.
At the cross I bow my

*This song is included on the companion recording. Intro on recording is 6 measures.

Copyright © 2006 Hillsong Publishing (APRA) (adm. in the US and Canada
at EMICMGPublishing.com). All rights reserved. Used by permission.

9

The Stand*

Gen. 1; Isa. 53:3-6; Rom. 12:1

J. H.   ♩ = ca. 70   JOEL HOUSTON

1. You stood be - fore   cre - a - tion,   e -
2. You stood be - fore   my fail - ure,   and
(3.) I'll walk up - on   sal - va - tion,   Your

ter - ni - ty   in   Your hand.   My
car - ried the cross   for   my shame.   My
Spir - it a - live in   me.   My

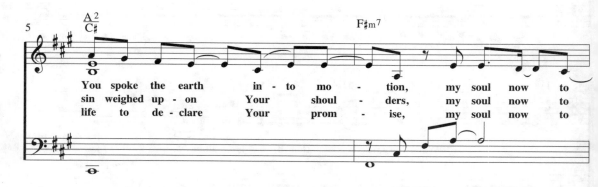

You spoke the earth   in - to mo - tion,   my soul now   to
sin weighed up - on   Your   shoul - ders, my soul now   to
life   to de - clare Your   prom - ise,   my soul now   to

stand.
stand.
stand.

*This song is included on the companion recording. Intro on recording is 8 measures.

Copyright © 2005 Hillsong Publishing (APRA) (adm. in the US and Canada at EMICMGPublishing.com) All rights reserved. Used by permission.

All   I am   is Yours.

All   I   am   is Yours.

Marvelous Light*
John 14:6; Eph. 5:8; 1 Pet. 2:9

C. H.

CHARLIE HALL

In - to mar - vel - ous   light   I'm   run - ning;   Out of dark - ness,

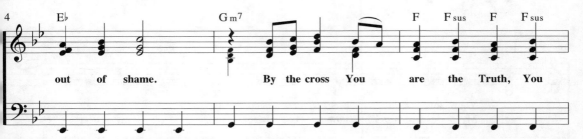

out   of   shame.   By   the cross   You   are   the   Truth,   You

10

*This song is included on the companion recording. Intro on recording is 10 measures.

Copyright © 2005 worshiptogether.com Songs (ASCAP) sixsteps Music (ASCAP)
(adm. at EMICMGPublishing.com) All rights reserved. Used by permission.

*NOTE: Men sing melody and Ladies sing harmonies on the recordings from measures 56-65.

11
You Never Let Go*

Pss. 23:4; 27:1; Hab. 3:17-19; 1 John 4:18

B. R. and M. R.

BETH REDMAN
and MATT REDMAN

1. E - ven though I walk through the val - ley of the
(2. I can see a) light that is com - ing for the

shad - ow of death, Your per - fect love is cast - ing out fear.
heart that holds on, A glo - rious light be - yond all com - pare.

And e - ven when I'm caught in the mid - dle of the
And there will be an end to these trou - bles, but un -

storms of this life, I won't turn back, I know You are near.
til that day comes, We'll live to know You here on the earth.

*This song is included on the companion recording. Intro on recording is 8 measures.

Copyright © 2005 Thankyou Music (PRS) (adm. worldwide at EMICMGPublishing.com)
excluding Europe which is adm. by Kingswaysongs). All rights reserved. Used by permission.

*NOTE: Melody sung an octave lower on recordings from measures 30-34.
Men sing melody and Ladies sing harmonies on the recordings from measures 35-37.

12 How He Loves*

Zech. 8:2; 1 John 3:1

J. M. M.

JOHN MARK MCMILLIAN

He is jea-lous for me, loves like a hur-ri-cane,

I am a tree Bend-ing be-neath the

weight of His wind and mer-cy. When

*This song is included on the companion recording. Intro on recording is 16 measures.

© 2005 Integrity's Hosanna! Music/ASCAP (adm. at EMICMGPublishing.com).
All rights reserved. Used by permission.

How Great Is Your Love*

1 John 3:1

D. C. and N. R.

DAVE CLARK and
NICK ROBINSON

*This song is included on the companion recording. Intro on recording is 8 measures.

© 2007 Pilot point Music (ASCAP) (admin. by Music Services)/New Spring Publishing (ASCAP)/
Callender Lane Music (ASCAP) (All rights for the world on behalf of Callender Lane Music
administered by New Spring Publishing)/Sunday Best Music (ASCAP). All rights reserved.

14 God of This City*

Exod. 15:11; Isa. 43:19

A. B., P. C., R. B.,
P. K., A. M. and I. J.

AARON BOYD, PETER COMFORT,
RICHARD BLEAKLEY, PETER KERNAGHAN,
ANDREW McCANN, IAN JORDAN

You're the God of this cit-y, You're the King of these

peo-ple, You're the Lord of this na-tion, You are.

You're the Light in this dark-ness, You're the Hope to the

hope-less, You're the Peace to the rest-less, You are.

*This song is included on the companion recording. Intro on recording is 4 measures.

Copyright © 2008 worshiptogether.com Songs (ASCAP) sixsteps Music (ASCAP)
(adm. at EMICMGPublishing.com) All rights reserved. Used by permission.

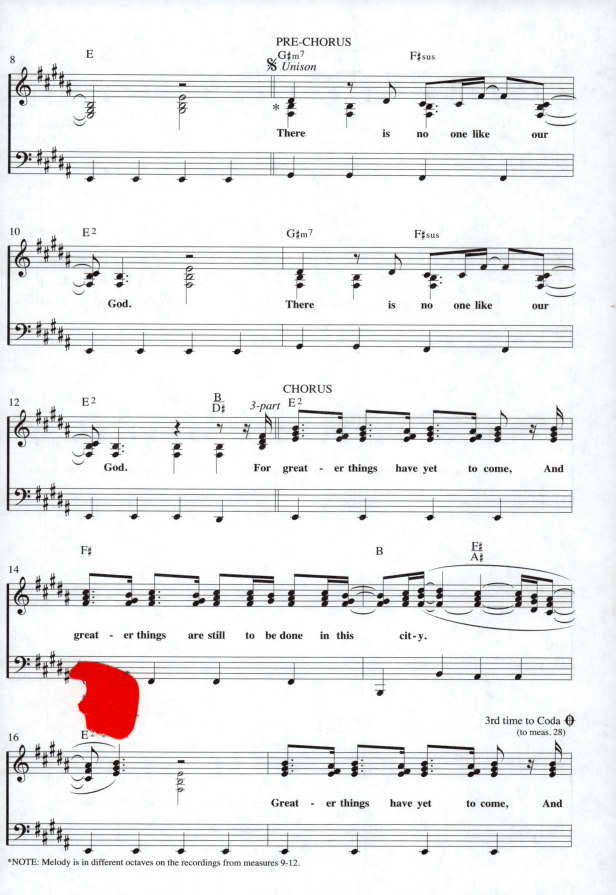

15 Meet with Me*

2 Chron. 7:1-2

LAMONT HIEBERT

L. H. ♩ = ca. 92

VERSE — *Unison*
I'm here to meet with You, come and meet with me. I'm here to find You, re-veal Your-self to me. As I wait,

CHORUS — *3-part*
You make me strong. As I long, You draw me to

This song is included on the companion recording. Intro on recording is 4 measures.

Copyright © 1999 Universal Music-Brentwood Benson Publishing (Maranatha)/ASCAP.
All rights reserved. Used by permission.

16 Come Thou Fount, Come Thou King*

Ps. 40:1-3; James 1:17

Trad. and T. M.

Traditional and
THOMAS MILLER

1. Come, Thou Fount of ev-'ry bless - ing, tune my heart to sing Thy
(2. I was) lost in ut - ter dark - ness 'til You came and res - cued
(3. O to) grace, how great a debt - or dai - ly I'm con - strained to

grace; Streams of mer - cy, nev - er ceas - ing, call for
me; I was bound by all my sin when Your love
be; Let Thy good - ness like a fet - ter bind my

*This song is included on the companion recording. Intro on recording is 8 measures.

© 2005 Gateway Create Publishing/BMI (adm. at EMICMGPublishing.com).
All rights reserved. Used by permission.

*NOTE: The arrangement can end on the downbeat of measure 39 OR can continue on.

17 When Amidst the Storm I'm Shaken

Matt. 8:23-27; 1 John 4:18

A. L.

ALLIE LAPOINTE

VERSE
1. When a-midst the storm I'm shak-en, wea-ried by the wind and waves; Lord, with-in me, faith a-wak-en; Je-sus, hear me call Your name.
3. Of-ten en-ters fear so sub-tle, weak-en-ing where once was love. For de-spair, trade hope e-ter-nal; for doubt, ex-change on-ly trust.

VERSE
2. Not to take a-way the tur-moil, not to change the
4. When my faith is firm-ly plant-ed, root-ed in sal-

© 2008 Consuming Worship Songs/BMI (admin. by Music Services). All rights reserved.

18   Sweetly Broken*

Gal. 2:20; 6:14

J. R.

JEREMY RIDDLE

1. To the cross I look and to the cross I

cling. Of its suf - f'ing I do

drink, of its work I do

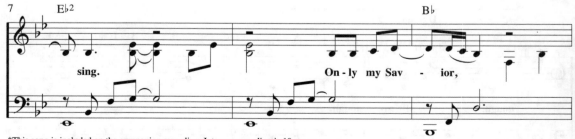

sing. On - ly my Sav - ior,

*This song is included on the companion recording. Intro on recording is 10 measures.

Copyright © 2005 Vineyard Music USA /ASCAP (admin. by Music Services).
All rights reserved. Used by permission.

You called me out of death,

You called me in-to life;

And I was un-der Your wrath,

now through the cross I'm re-con-ciled.

(to meas. 17)

2 BRIDGE

Unison

In awe of the cross I must con-fess,

*NOTE: Melody sung an octave lower on the recordings from measures 45-52.

Hear Us from Heaven*

2 Chron. 7:13-16

J. A.

JARED ANDERSON

*This song is included on the companion recording. Intro on recording is 4 measures.

Copyright © 2004 Vertical Worship Songs/ASCAP (adm. at EMICMGPublishing.com).
All rights reserved. Used by permission.

19

20 Cannons*

Ps. 19:1; Isa. 6:3-5; Rev. 4:11

P. W.

PHIL WICKHAM

♩ = ca. 78

VERSE *Unison*

1. It's fall - ing from the clouds, a strange and love - ly sound; I
2. Beau - ti - ful and free, the song of gal - ax - ies,

hear it in the thun - der and the rain. It's
Reach - ing far be - yond the Milk - y Way. Let's

ring - ing in the skies, like can - nons in the night; The
join in with the sound, come on, let's sing it out; As the

mu - sic of the un - i - verse plays. We're sing - ing,
mu - sic of the un - i - verse plays.

3-part

*This song is included on the companion recording. Intro on recording is 8 measures.

© 2007 Seems Like Music & Phil Wickham Music/BMI.
All rights admin. by Simpleville Music, Inc. Used by permission.

Came to My Rescue*

Ps. 40:1-3

21

M. S., J. D. and D. T.

MARTY SAMPSON, JOEL DAVIES
and DYLAN THOMAS

1. Fall - ing on my knees in wor - ship,
2. My whole life I place in Your hands.

giv - ing all I am to seek Your face;
God of mer - cy, hum - bled I bow down

Lord, all I am is Yours.
in Your pres - ence at Your throne.

*This song is included on the companion recording. Intro on recording is 8 measures.

Copyright © 2005 Hillsong Publishing (APRA) (adm. in the US and Canada
at EMICMGPublishing.com) All rights reserved. Used by permission.

22

For All You've Done*

Ps. 40:1-3; John 1:14; Heb. 10:19-23

R. M.

REUBEN MORGAN

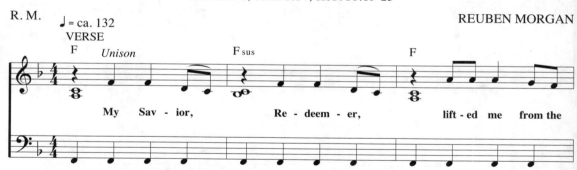

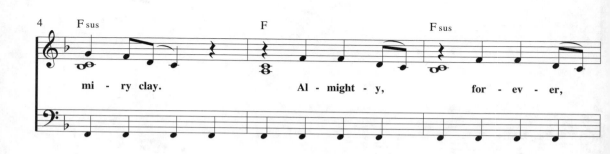

*This song is included on the companion recording. Intro on recording is 8 measures.

Copyright © 2004 Hillsong Publishing (APRA) (adm. in the US and Canada
at EMICMGPublishing.com) All rights reserved. Used by permission.

Hal - le - lu - jah for all You've done.

A Mighty Fortress*   23

Ps. 46:1-3; Heb. 12:28-29; Rev. 11:15

C. N. and N. N.

CHRISTY NOCKELS
and NATHAN NOCKELS

♩ = ca. 72 VERSE

1st time: Unison
2nd time: 2-part

1. Our God is a con - sum - ing fire, a burn - ing ho - ly
(2. Our) God is jeal - ous for His own, none could com - pre -

flame with glo - ry and free - dom. Our
- hend His love and His mer - cy. Our

*This song is included on the companion recording. Intro on recording is 8 measures.

Copyright © 2009 worshiptogether.com Songs (ASCAP) sixsteps Music (ASCAP)
Sweater Weather Music (ASCAP) (adm. at EMICMGPublishing.com)
All rights reserved. Used by permission.

Glorious*

Isa. 6:1-5; Rev. 5:11-14

B. B. and P. B.

♩ = ca. 102

BRENTON BROWN
and PAUL BALOCHE

1. Look in-side the mys-t'ry,
2. Look be-yond the tomb-stone,

see the emp-ty cross;
see the liv-ing God;

See the ris-en Sav-ior,
See the res-ur-rec-ted

vic-

to-ri-ous and strong.
Rul-er of my heart.

*This song is included on the companion recording. Intro on recording is 8 measures.

Copyright © 2009 Thankyou Music (PRS) (adm. worldwide at EMICMGPublishing.com
excluding Europe which is adm. by Kingswaysongs)/
Integrity's Hosanna! Music (ASCAP)/ Leadworship Songs (ASCAP)
(adm. at EMICMGPublishing.com). All rights reserved. Used by permission.

25 You Are God Alone (Not a God)*

Isa. 40:12-26

B. J. F. and C. F.

BILLY J. FOOTE
and CINDY FOOTE

♩ = ca. 70
VERSE

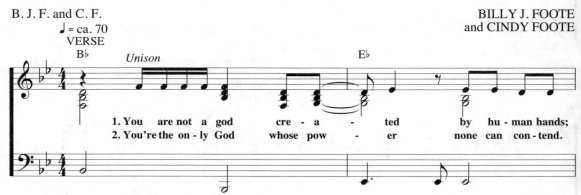

1. You are not a god cre - a - ted by hu - man hands;
2. You're the on - ly God whose pow - er none can con - tend.

*This song is included on the companion recording. Intro on recording is 8 measures.

© 2004 Billy Foote Music (ASCAP)/ Integrity's Hosanna! Music (ASCAP)
(adm. by EMICMGPublishing.com). All rights reserved. Used by permission.

26 Our Great God*

Ps. 48:1; Matt. 11:28-30; Luke 15:10-32; Rom. 8:1

N. R. and A. L.

NICK ROBERTSON
and ALLIE LAPOINTE

1. You pur-sue the pro-di-gal,
2. You for-give a-gain and a-gain,

You re-deem the years of re-gret;
You re-joice when hearts turn to You;

You re-new the burned out, bro-ken,
There is no con-dem-na-tion,

wear-y souls in need of rest.
an-y-one in Christ is made new.

*This song is included on the companion recording. Intro on recording is 8 measures.

© 2011 Pilot Point Music/ASCAP and PsalmSinger Music/BMI
(both admin. by Music Services). All rights reserved.

27 Jesus Saves*

Isa. 53:4-6; Matt. 2:1-11; Luke 2:8-20; Acts 4:12; Rev. 14:1-3

D. M. and T. C.

DAVID MOFFITT and
TRAVIS COTTRELL

*This song is included on the companion recording. Intro on recording is 8 measures.

Copyright © 2007 New Spring Publishing (ASCAP)/
First Hand Revelation (ASCAP) (admin. by The Loving Company).
All rights reserved. Used by permission.

Not Just a Story

28

Ps. 139:7-12; Jer. 23:23-24; Acts 17:28

R. F. and S. M.

RICHIE FIKE and
SEAN MULHOLLAND

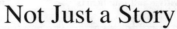

© 2009 PsalmSinger Music (BMI) (admin. by Music Services)/Brave World Publishing (BMI)
(admin. by Lillenas Publishing Company c/o Music Services). All rights reserved.

Come, People of the Risen King*

Pss. 23:6; 136:1; 1 Pet. 1:3

29

K. L. G., S. T. and K. G.

KRISTYN LENNOX GETTY,
STUART TOWNEND and KEITH GETTY

1. Come, peo - ple of the ris - en King who de -
(2. Come,) those whose joy is morn - ing sun and those
(3. Come,) young and old from ev - 'ry land, men and

light to bring Him praise. Come all and tune your
weep - ing through the night. Come those who tell of
wo - men of the faith. Come those with full or

hearts to sing to the Morn - ing Star of Grace. From the
bat - tles won and those strug - gling in the fight. For His
emp - ty hands, find the rich - es of His grace. O - ver

shift - ing shad - ows of the earth we will lift our eyes to
per - fect love will nev - er change and His mer - cies nev - er
all the world His peo - ple sing, shore to shore we hear them

*This song is included on the companion recording. Intro on recording is 8 measures.

Copyright © 2009 Thankyou Music (PRS) (adm. worldwide at EMICMGPublishing.com)
excluding Europe which is adm. by Kingswaysongs). All rights reserved. Used by permission.

30 Glorious Day (Living He Loved Me)*

John 1:14; Gal. 4:4-5; 1 Thess. 4:13-18; 1 Tim. 3:16

M. H. and M. B.

♩ = ca. 76

MARK HALL and
MICHAEL BLEAKER

*This song is included on the companion recording. Intro on recording is 4 measures.

Copyright © 2009 My Refuge Music (BMI) (adm. at EMICMGPublishing.com)/
Word Music, LLC. (ASCAP)/Sony/Atv Tree Pub (BMI).
All rights reserved. Used by permission.

31   Song of Hope (Heaven Came Down)*

Eph. 5:8; Titus 3:3-7

R. S., R. O., D. H.,
T. J., C. J. and T. T.
♩ = ca. 116
VERSE

ROBBIE SEAY, RYAN OTIS,
DAN HAMILTON, TAYLOR JOHNSON,
CHASE JENKINS and TED TYORNHOM

1. All things bright and beau-ti-ful You are. All things wise and won-der-ful You are.
2. All things new; I can start a-gain. Cre-a-tor God, call-ing me Your friend.

*This song is included on the companion recording. Intro on recording is 8 measures.

Copyright © 2007 Birdwing Music (ASCAP)/Meaux Hits (ASCAP)/
Tedasia Music (ASCAP) (adm. at EMICMGPublishing.com).
All rights reserved. Used by permission.

1st time: Bass whole notes

32 Amazed*

Pss. 73:23-28; 149:2-5; Zeph. 3:17; Eph. 3:14-19

J. A.

JARED ANDERSON

1. You dance o - ver me while I
(2. You paint) the morn - ing sky with mir -

am un - a - ware. You sing all a - round
- a - cles in mind. My hope will al - ways stand

but I nev - er hear the sound.
for You hold me in Your hand.

Lord, I'm a - mazed by You.

*This song is included on the companion recording. Intro on recording is 8 measures.

© 2003 Vertical Worship Songs/ASCAP (adm. at EMICMGPublishing.com).
All rights reserved. Used by permission.

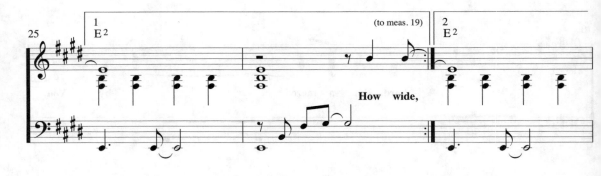

How wide,

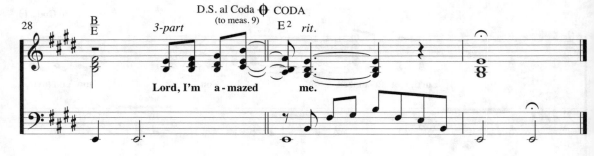

D.S. al Coda CODA
(to meas. 9)

3-part

Lord, I'm a-mazed me.

33

Desert Song*

Ps. 42-43; Isa. 54:16-17;Rom. 8:35-37; 1 Pet. 1:6-7

B. F. ♩ = ca. 110

BROOKE FRASER

VERSE

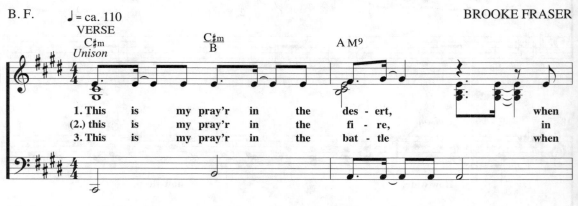

1. This is my pray'r in the des - ert,
(2.) this is my pray'r in the fi - re,
3. This is my pray'r in the bat - tle when

all that's with - in me feels dry.
weak - ness or tri - al or pain.
tri - umph is still on its way.

*This song is included on the companion recording. Intro on recording is 8 measures.

Copyright © 2007 Hillsong Publishing (APRA) (adm. in the US and Canada
at EMICMGPublishing.com). All rights reserved. Used by permission.

D.S. al Coda ⊕ CODA

3-part (to meas. 10)

I will bring here!"

VERSE

Unison

4. This is my pray'r in the har - vest, when

fa - vor and prov - i - dence flow.

I know I'm filled to be emp - tied a - gain. The

seed I've re - ceived I will sow.

34 Remember and Proclaim

Matt. 11:28-30; 1 Cor. 11:23-26

M. L. and W. W.

MATHEW LINTON
and WENDY WILLS

1. This bread, His flesh, this wine, His blood; Em-blems of the love of God. We fear no wrath or pierc-ing sword; We are re-deemed, re-leased, re-

2. Come ev-'ry soul weighted down with care; Anx-ious thoughts, un-eas-y prayers. Come and be-lieve and find your rest; Come and re-ceive the righ-teous-

© 2005 Consuming Praise Songs/ASCAP and Consuming Worship Songs/BMI
(both admin. by Music Services). All rights reserved.

35

Because He Lives

John 14:19; Gal. 4:4-5

GLORIA GAITHER and W. J. G.   WILLIAM J. GAITHER

Copyright © 1971 Gaither Music Company/ASCAP, Hanna Street Music/BMI.
All rights controlled by Gaither Copyright Management. Used by permission.

A New Hallelujah*

Ps. 98; Acts 1:8

D. S., M. W. S. and P. B.

DEBBY SMITH, MICHAEL W. SMITH
and PAUL BALOCHE

*This song is included on the companion recording. Intro on recording is 12 measures.

© 2008 and this arrangement © 2011 Smittfly Music (ASCAP) (admin. by Word Music, LLC)/
Word Music, LLC (ASCAP)/Integrity's Hosanna! Music (ASCAP)/Leadership Songs (ASCAP)/
This Is Your Time Music (ASCAP) (adm. at EMICMGPublishing.com).
All rights reserved. International copyright secured. Used by permission.

37

Send the Water

Ps. 51:1-2; John 4:1-42

T. B. and M. H.

TRACEY BAKER
and MARK HARRIS

1. There came a wo-man to the well;
(2. Deep) is the sor-row of my sin;

deep-est pain the Sav-ior felt.
yet some-how I search with-in;

spoke of ev-er-last-ing life;
find no so-lace in my soul,

well that nev-er would run dry.
emp-ti-ness and bit-ter cold.

Her
And

He
I

A
Just

She
I

© 2010 Consuming Praise Songs (ASCAP) (Administered by Music Services)/
Coastal Lyric Music (ASCAP). All Rights Reserved.

1

Come and make me whole.

2. Deep

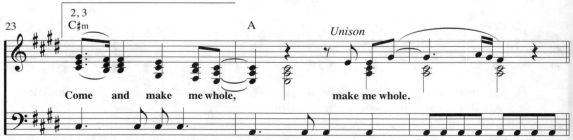

2, 3

Come and make me whole, make me whole.

Unison

BRIDGE

All my guilt and all my shame, all my sin, the deep - est stains;

Wash a-way, wash a-way.

All my guilt and all my shame, all my sin, the deep - est stains;

38

Jesus Messiah*

John 8:12; 2 Cor. 5:21; Phil. 2:5-11; Col. 1:27

J. R., D. C., C. T. and E. C.

JESSE REEVES, DANIEL CARSON,
CHRIS TOMLIN, ED CASH

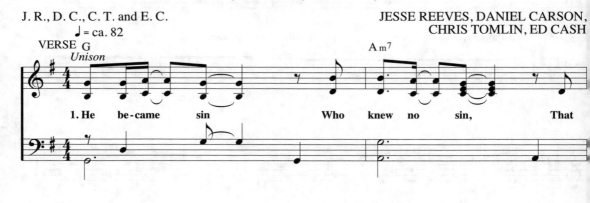

1. He be-came sin Who knew no sin, That

we might be-come His righ-teous-ness. He

hum-bled Him-self and car-ried the cross;

Love so a-maz-ing, love so a-

*This song is included on the companion recording. Intro on recording is 4 measures.

Copyright © 2008 worshiptogether.com Songs (ASCAP)/sixsteps Music (ASCAP)/
Vamos Publishing (ASCAP) (adm. at EMICMGPublishing.com)/Alletrop Music (BMI)
(admin. by Music Services). All rights reserved. Used by permission.

39   O Worship the King*

Ps. 104:1-4; Dan. 7:9

CHRIS TOMLIN

*This song is included on the companion recording. Intro on recording is 12 measures.

Copyright © 2004 worshiptogether.com Songs (ASCAP) sixsteps Music (ASCAP)
(adm. at EMICMGPublishing.com) All rights reserved. Used by permission.

All of My Life

Pss. 27:4; 42:1; 63:1

40

C. H.

CASSIDY HARRIS

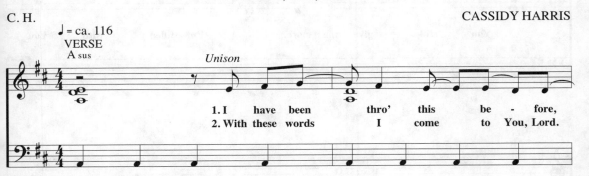

1. I have been thro' this be - fore,
2. With these words I come to You, Lord.

Pu - ri - fy
Hum - ble ser -

my heart a - gain.
- vant, here I am.

When I am dry, You give me more. When I am full,

© 2001 Pilot Point Music/ASCAP (admin. by Music Services). All rights reserved.

41

Salvation Is Here*

John 14:19; Acts 4:12

J. H.

JOEL HOUSTON

♩ = ca. 116

VERSE

1st time: Unison
2nd time: 2-part

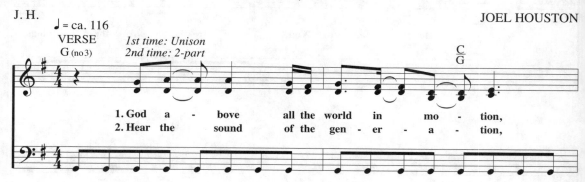

1. God a - bove all the world in mo - tion,
2. Hear the sound of the gen - er - a - tion,

God a - bove all my hopes and fears;
mak - ing loud our free - dom song;

I don't care what the world throws at me now,
All in all, that the world will know Your name,

I'm gon - na be al - right. 'Cause I
we're gon - na be al - right.

*This song is included on the companion recording. Intro on recording is 10 measures.

Copyright © 2004 Hillsong Publishing (APRA) (adm. in the US and Canada at EMICMGPublishing.com). All rights reserved. Used by permission.

'cause You are a-live and You live in me.

42 Let God Arise*

Ps. 68:1-4; 1 Cor. 15:54-57; Rev. 1:17-18; 11:15

J. R., C. T. and E. C.

JESSE REEVES, CHRIS TOMLIN
and ED CASH

♩ = ca. 144
Unison

VERSE

1. Hear the ho - ly roar of God re - sound,
(2. His en) - e - mies will run for sure;

Watch the wa -
And the church

- ters part be - fore us now.
will stand, she will en - dure.

*This song is included on the companion recording. Intro on recording is 8 measures.

Copyright © 2006 worshiptogether.com Songs (ASCAP)/sixsteps Music (ASCAP)/
Vamos Publishing (ASCAP) (adm. at EMICMGPublishing.com)/Alletrop Music (BMI)
(admin. by Music Services). All rights reserved. Used by permission.

Awesome Is the Lord Most High* 43

Pss. 47:1-2; 86:10; 145:3

C. P., C. T., J. R. and J. A.

CARY PIERCE, CHRIS TOMLIN,
JESSE REEVES and JON ABEL

*This song is included on the companion recording. Intro on recording is 8 measures.

Copyright © 2005 Bridge Building Music (BMI)/45 Degrees Music (BMI)/Popular Purple Publishing (BMI)
(All rights for 45 Degrees Music & Popular Purple Music admin. by Bridge Building Music)/
worshiptogether.com songs (ASCAP)/sixsteps Music (ASCAP)/Vamos Publishing (ASCAP)
(adm. at EMICMGPublishing.com). All rights reserved. Used by permission.

44 Nothing but the Blood*

Heb. 9:11-14; 12:22-24

M. R.

MATT REDMAN

1. Your blood speaks a bet-ter word than all the emp-ty claims
(2. Your) cross tes-ti-fies in grace; tells of the Fa-ther's heart

I've heard up-on this earth; Speaks righ-teous-ness for me
to make a way for us. Now bold-ly we ap-proach,

and stands in my de-fense; Je-sus, it's Your blood.
not earth-ly con-fi-dence; It's on-ly by Your blood.

What can wash a-way

*This song is included on the companion recording. Intro on recording is 6 measures.

Copyright © 2004 Thankyou Music (PRS) (adm. worldwide at EMICMGPublishing.com
excluding Europe which is adm. by Kingswaysongs).
All rights reserved. Used by permission.

O My Lord

Eph. 2:14-18; Titus 3:3-7; 1 John 3:1; 4:9-10

45

J. W.

JEROD WILSON

© 2008 Consuming Worship Songs/BMI (admin. by Music Services). All rights reserved.

I find the peace shed by the blood of the Lamb.
More beau - ti - ful than eyes can see.

CHORUS

O my Lord, let mer -
- cy come; Come and lead me on.
O my Lord, let mer -
- cy come; Come and lead

46 Sing Sing Sing*

Ps. 98:1-4; Acts 4:12; Phil. 2:9-11

J. R., D. C., C. T., T. N. and M. G.

JESSE REEVES, DANIEL CARSON,
CHRIS TOMLIN, TRAVIS NUNN,
and MATT GILDER

♩ = ca. 148

Unison (opt. 2-part) CHORUS

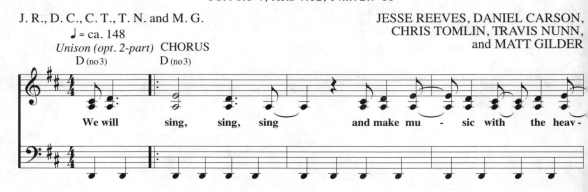

We will sing, sing, sing and make mu - sic with the heav-

-ens, We will sing, sing, sing, grate - ful that You hear

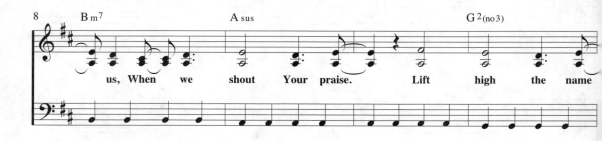

us, When we shout Your praise. Lift high the name

of Je - sus.

*This song is included on the companion recording. Intro on recording is 1.5 measures.

Copyright © 2008 worshiptogether.com Songs (ASCAP)/sixsteps Music (ASCAP)/
Vamos Publishing (ASCAP) (adm. at EMICMGPublishing.com)/Ryan House Music (BMI)
(admin. by Music Services). All rights reserved. Used by permission.

*NOTE: Men sing melody and Ladies sing harmonies on the recordings from measures 41-55.

47 Healer*

Exod. 11:26; Isa. 43:2-5; Matt. 19:26; 2 Pet. 1:3

M. G.

MIKE GUGLIELMUCCI

*This song is included on the companion recording. Intro on recording is 8 measures.

Copyright © 2007 Planet Shakers Publishing (ASCAP).
All rights administered in North and South America by Music Services, Inc.,
www.musicservices.org. All rights reserved. Used by permission.

Ascend to Heaven*

Exod. 19:10, 20-22; Isa. 6:1; Matt. 17:1-8; Acts 4:12

48

R. F. and S. M.

RICHIE FIKE and
SEAN MULHOLLAND

*This song is included on the companion recording. Intro on recording is 8 measures.

© 2009 First Sunday Music (ASCAP) (adm. by Sunday Best Music)/
Pilot Point Music (ASCAP) (adm. by Music Services)/Brave World Publishing
(adm. by Lillenas Publishing Company c/o Music Services). All rights reserved. Used by permission.

49 No Sweeter Name*

John 14:6; Phil. 2:9-11

K. J.

KARI JOBE

*This song is included on the companion recording. Intro on recording is 8 measures.

Copyright © 2004 Integrity's Praise! Music (BMI)/Gateway Create Publishing (BMI)
(adm. at EMICMGPublishing.com). All rights reserved. Used by permission.

Lead Me to the Cross*

Gal. 2:20; 6:14; Phil. 3:7-11

B. F.

BROOKE FRASER

1. Sav - ior, I come, qui - et my soul,
2. You were as I, tempt - ed and tried

re - mem - ber
hu - man;

*This song is included on the companion recording. Intro on recording is 4 measures.

Copyright © 2004 Hillsong Publishing (APRA) (adm. in the US and Canada
at EMICMGPublishing.com). All rights reserved. Used by permission.

I Will Boast*

Jer. 9:23-24; 1 Cor. 1:26-31; Gal. 6:14; Rev. 5:12-14

P. B.

PAUL BALOCHE

Let not the wise man boast in his wis - dom or the strong

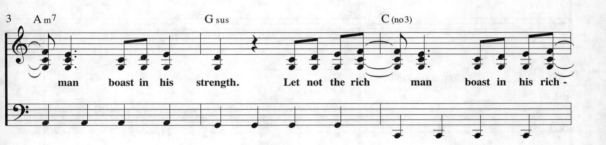

man boast in his strength. Let not the rich man boast in his rich -

- es, but let the hum - ble come and give thanks to the

One who made us, the One who saved us.

*This song is included on the companion recording. Intro on recording is 8 measures.

© 2006 Integrity's Hosanna! Music/ASCAP (adm. at EMICMGPublishing.com).
All rights reserved. Used by permission.

52

I'll Fly Away

1 Thess. 4:16-18

A. E. B.

ALBERT E. BRUMLEY

1. Some glad morn-ing when this life is o'er, I'll fly a-way;
2. When the shad-ows of this life have gone, I'll fly a-way;
3. Just a few more wear-y days and then, I'll fly a-way;

To a home on God's ce-les-tial shore,
Life a bird from pris-on bars has flown,
To a land where joys shall nev-er end,

I'll fly a-way.
I'll fly a-way.
I'll fly a-way.

Copyright © 1938 by E. M. Bartlett. Copyright renewed 1966 by Mrs. E.M. Bartlett.
Assigned to Albert E. Brumley & Sons/SESAC (admin. ClearBox Rights).
All rights reserved. Used by permission.

53 Overcome*

Matt. 28:18; Rev. 5:12-14; 12:11; 17:14

J. E.   ♩. = ca. 48

JON EGAN

1. Seat-ed a-bove, en-throned in the Fa-ther's love;
2. God's on-ly Son, per-fect and spot-less One;
3. Pow-er in hand, speak-ing the Fa-ther's plan;

Des-tined to die, poured out for all man-
He nev-er sinned but suf-fered as if He
Send-ing us out, light in this bro-ken

kind.
did.
land.

All au-thor-i-ty, ev-'ry vic-to-ry is

thor-i-ty, ev-'ry vic-to-ry is

PRE-CHORUS

*This song is included on the companion recording. Intro on recording is 12 measures.

Copyright © 2007 Vertical Worship Songs/ASCAP (adm. at EMICMGPublishing.com).
All rights reserved. Used by permission.

Healing Is in Your Hands

Rom. 8:35-39

54

C. T., M. R., D. C.,
C. N. and N. N.

CHRIS TOMLIN, MATT REDMAN,
DANIEL CARSON, CHRISTY NOCKELS
and NATHAN NOCKELS

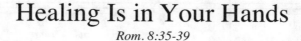

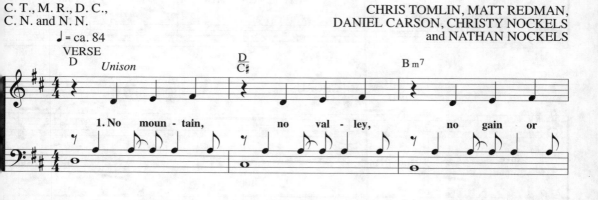

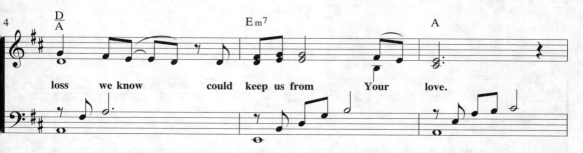

Copyright © 2010 Thankyou Music (PRS) (adm. worldwide at EMICMGPublishing.com excluding
Europe which is adm. by Kingswaysongs/worshiptogether.com Songs (ASCAP)/sixsteps Music (ASCAP)/
Vamos Publishing (ASCAP)/Sweater Weather Music (ASCAP)/Said And Done Music (ASCAP)
(adm. at EMICMGPublishing.com). All rights reserved. Used by permission.

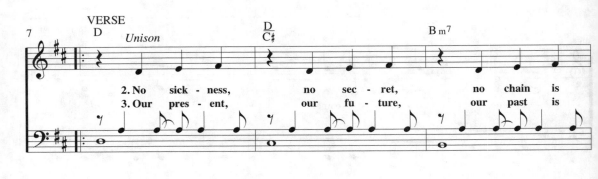

VERSE
Unison

2. No sick - ness, no se - cret, no chain is
3. Our pres - ent, our fu - ture, our past is

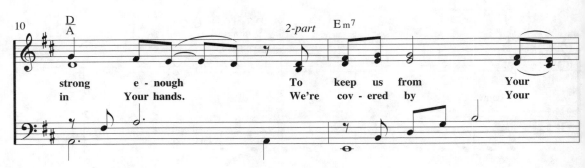

2-part

strong   e - nough   To   keep us from   Your
in   Your hands.   We're cov - ered by   Your

love,   to   keep us from   Your
blood,   we're cov - ered by   Your

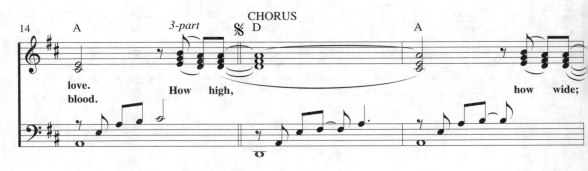

3-part   **CHORUS**

love.   How high,   how wide;
blood.

No mat - ter where   I   am

God You Reign*

Isa. 40:12-26; 52:7

L. B. and M. F.

♩ = ca. 90

LINCOLN BREWSTER
and MIA FIELDS

VERSE

1. You paint the night, You count the stars
2. You part the seas, You move the moun-

-tains with the words that You say. My song re-mains,

and You call them by name. The skies pro-claim,

God You reign.
God You reign.

Your glo- ry shines, You teach the sun
You hold my life, You know my heart

*This song is included on the companion recording. Intro on recording is 8 measures.

Copyright © 2008 Shout! Publishing (ASCAP) (adm. in the US and Canada
at EMICMGPublishing.com)/Integrity's Hosanna! Music (ASCAP)
(adm. at EMICMGPublishing.com). All rights reserved. Used by permission.

56 Today Is the Day*

Ps. 118:24; Phil. 3:12-14

L. B. and P. B.

LINCOLN BREWSTER
and PAUL BALOCHE

1. I'm cast - ing my cares a - side, I'm leav - ing my past
(2. I'm put - ting my fears) a - side, I'm leav - ing my doubts

be - hind. I'm set - ting my heart and mind on You,
be - hind. I'm giv - ing my hopes and dreams to You,

Je - sus. I'm reach - ing my hands
Je - sus.

to Yours, Be - liev - ing there's so

*This song is included on the companion recording. Intro on recording is 12 measures.

© 2008 Integrity's Praise! Music (BMI)/Integrity's Hosanna! Music (ASCAP)/Leadworship Songs (ASCAP) (adm. at EMICMGPublishing.com). All Rights Reserved. Used By Permission.

Today is the day.

57   Your God Will Come*
Isa. 35

N. R.

NICK ROBERTSON

1. Strength-en the fee - ble hands and
2. O God of A - bra - ham, in the

stead - y the knees that give way. Say to
midst of the dark - ness shine. Make the

those with fear - ful hearts, "Be
des - ert to live a - gain; show - er

*This song is included on the companion recording. Intro on recording is 5 measures.

© 2010 Sunday Best Music/ASCAP. All rights reserved. Used by permission.

*NOTE: Men sing melody and Ladies sing harmonies on the recordings from measures 19-26.

58

Your Love Never Fails*

Ps. 30:5; Lam. 3:22-23; Rom. 8:28, 35-39; Heb. 13:8

C. M. and A. S.

CHRIS MCCLARNEY and
ANTHONY SKINNER

1. Noth - ing can sep - a - rate e - ven if I ran a - way, Your love nev - er fails.

(1) I know I still make mis - takes, but You have new mer - cies for me
(2) The cha - sm is far too wide, I nev - er thought I'd reach the

*This song is included on the companion recording. Intro on recording is 8 measures.

Copyright © 2009 Thankyou Music (PRS) (adm. worldwide at EMICMGPublishing.com
excluding Europe which is adm. by Kingswaysongs)/Integrity's Alleluia! Music (SESAC)/
Out Of The Cave Music (SESAC) (adm. at EMICMGPublishing.com). All rights reserved. Used by permission.

59

God Is Great*

Ps. 145:3-7; Isa. 6:3; John 4:23-24

M. S.

MARTY SAMPSON

Verse

1. All cre-a-tion cries to You,
2. All cre-a-tion gives You praise,
3. All to You, O God, we bring,

wor-ship-ing in Spir-it and in truth.
You a-lone are tru-ly great.
Je-sus, teach us how to live.

Glo-ry to
You a-lone
Let Your fi-

the Faith-ful One,
are God who reigns
-re burn in us

Je-sus Christ, God's Son.
that

*This song is included on the companion recording. Intro on recording is 8 measures.

Copyright © 2001 Hillsong Publishing (APRA) (adm. in the US and Canada
at EMICMGPublishing.com) All rights reserved. Used by permission.

60

None but Jesus*

Pss. 37:4; 63:1, 6-7; 91:1-2

B. F.

BROOKE FRASER

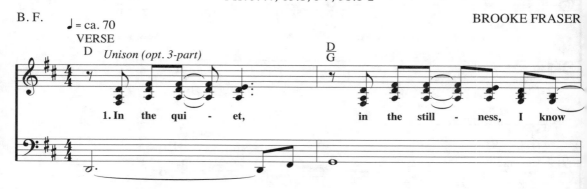

1. In the qui-et, in the still-ness, I know that You are God. In the se-cret

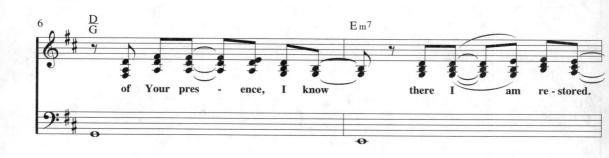

of Your pres-ence, I know there I am re-stored.

When You call, I won't re-fuse;

*This song is included on the companion recording. Intro on recording is 4 measures.

Copyright © 2007 Hillsong Publishing (APRA) (adm. in the US and Canada
at EMICMGPublishing.com). All rights reserved. Used by permission.

in con-fu - sion, I know You're sov - 'reign still.

In the mo - ment of my weak - ness, You give

me grace to do Your will. When You

call, I won't de - lay; This, my

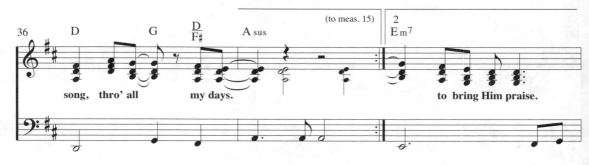

(to meas. 15)

song, thro' all my days. to bring Him praise.

61

The More I Seek You*

Ps. 63:1; Luke 10:38-42

Z. N.

ZACH NEESE

*This song is included on the companion recording. Intro on recording is 8 measures.

© 1999 Gateway Create Publishing and Integrity's Praise Songs/ASCAP
(both adm. at EMICMGPublishing.com). All rights reserved. Used by permission.

62 You Alone Can Rescue

Pss. 49:7-9; 107:10-16; Rom. 5:20; 1 Pet. 3:18-22

MATT REDMAN
and JONAS MYRIN

Who, O Lord, could save them - selves, their own soul could heal? Our shame was deep - er than the sea, Your grace is deep - er still. still. And You a - lone can

Copyright © 2009 Shout! Publishing (ASCAP) (adm. in the US and Canada at EMICMGPublishing.com)/
Thankyou Music (PRS) (adm. worldwide at EMICMGPublishing.com excluding Europe
which is adm. by Kingswaysongs)/worshiptogether.com Songs (ASCAP)/sixsteps Music (ASCAP)/
Said And Done Music (ASCAP) (adm. at EMICMGPublishing.com). All rights reserved. Used by permission.

63 Friend of God*

Ps. 8:3-4; John 15:13-15; James 2:23

I. H. and M. G.

ISRAEL HOUGHTON
and MICHAEL GUNGOR

Who am I that You are mind-ful of me,

that You hear me when I call?

Is it true that You are think-ing of

me? How You love me,

*This song is included on the companion recording. Intro on recording is 8 measures.

© 2003 Integrity's Praise! Music/BMI and Vertical Worship Songs/ASCAP
(adm. at EMICMGPublishing.com). All rights reserved. Used by permission.

One Way

John 14:6; Rom. 12:1; 2 Cor. 5:7; Heb. 13:8

64

J. H. and J. D.

♩ = ca. 148

JOEL HOUSTON and
JONATHAN DOUGLASS

1. I lay my life down at Your feet; You're the on - ly
2. You were al - ways, al - ways there, ev - 'ry "how" and

One I need. I turn to You and
ev - 'ry "where." Your grace a - bounds so

You are al - ways there.
deep - ly with - in me.

Copyright © 2003 Hillsong Publishing (APRA) (adm. in the US and Canada
at EMICMGPublishing.com). All rights reserved. Used by permission.

The Family of God

Rom. 8:16-17

WILLIAM J. GAITHER
and GLORIA GAITHER

WILLIAM J. GAITHER

Copyright © 1970 Gaither Music Company/ASCAP, Hanna Street Music/BMI.
All rights controlled by Gaither Copyright Management. Used by permission.

sod; For I'm part of the fam-'ly, the

fam-'ly of God.

66 Reverence Your Name

Ps. 34:1; Rom. 12:1; Heb. 4:14-16

E. T.

EON TROTMAN

I don't de-serve to be in Your pres - ence, Lord;

I don't de-serve to bow be-fore Your throne.

Copyright © 2007 by PsalmSinger Music/BMI (admin. by Music Services). All rights reserved.

67 From the Inside Out*

Pss. 103:1; 136:1

J. H.

JOEL HOUSTON

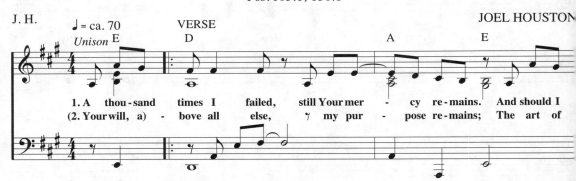

1. A thou-sand times I failed, still Your mer - cy re-mains. And should I
(2. Your will, a) - bove all else, my pur - pose re-mains; The art of

stum-ble a - gain, still I'm caught in Your grace. Ev-er-last-
los-ing my - self in bring - ing You praise.

-ing, Your light will shine when all else fades. Nev-er-end-

-ing, Your glo - ry goes be - yond all fame.

*This song is included on the companion recording. Intro on recording is 8 measures.

Copyright © 2005 Hillsong Publishing (APRA) (adm. in the US and Canada
at EMICMGPublishing.com) All rights reserved. Used by permission.

Great Is Thy Faithfulness

68

Lam. 3:22-23; James 1:17

THOMAS CHISHOLM

WILLIAM RUNYAN

1. Great is Thy faith-ful-ness, O God, my Fa-ther;
2. Sum-mer and win-ter, and spring-time and har-vest,
3. Par-don for sin and a peace that en-dur-eth,

There is no shad-ow of turn-ing with Thee.
Sun, moon, and stars in their cours-es a-bove,
Thy own dear pres-ence to cheer and to guide,

Thou chang-est not; Thy com-pas-sions, they fail not.
Join with all na-ture in man-i-fold wit-ness
Strength for to-day and bright hope for to-mor-row—

As Thou hast been Thou for-ev-er wilt be.
To Thy great faith-ful-ness, mer-cy, and love.
Bless-ings all mine, with ten thou-sand be-side!

Copyright © 1923. Renewal 1951 by Hope Publishing Co., Carol Stream, IL 60188.
All rights reserved. Used by permission.

69 My Savior, My God*

Acts 4:12; 1 Cor. 2:1-2; Gal. 6:14

A. S. and D. G.

AARON SHUST and
DORA GREENWELL

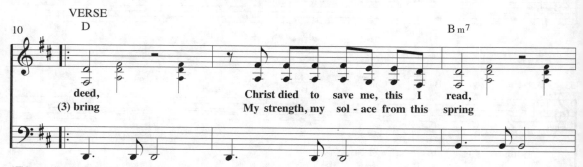

*This song is included on the companion recording. Intro on recording is 8 measures.

Copyright © 2005 Bridge Building Music (BMI)/White Spot Publishing (BMI).
All rights for the world on behalf of White Spot Publishing
administered by Bridge Building Music. All rights reserved. Used by permission

*NOTE: Men sing melody and Ladies sing harmonies on the recordings from measures 24-33.

Untitled Hymn
(Come to Jesus)

Matt. 11:28-30; Acts 4:12

CHRIS RICE

© 2003 Clumsy Fly Music/ASCAP (admin. by Word Music, LLC).
All rights reserved. Used by permission.

71 All Because of Jesus*

John 14:19; Acts 17:28; James 1:17

S. F.

STEVE FEE

Giv-er of ev - 'ry breath I breathe, Au-thor of all

e - ter - ni - ty, Giv-er of ev - 'ry per - fect thing,

to You be the glo - ry.

Mak-er of heav - en and of earth, No one can com-

*This song is included on the companion recording. Intro on recording is 7.5 measures.

Copyright © 2007 Worship Together Music (BMI)/Sixsteps Bmi Designee (BMI)/
Levi Bear Music (ASCAP) (adm. at EMICMGPublishing.com).
All rights reserved. Used by permission.

72

Glory to God Forever*

Rev. 1:8; 5:12-14

V. B. and S. F.

VICKY BEECHING
and STEVE FEE

1. Be - fore the world was made, be - fore You spoke it to be;
2. Cre - a - tor, God, You gave me breath so I could praise;

You were the King of kings, yeah, You were, yeah, You were.
Your great and match - less name all my days, all my days.

And now You're reign - ing still, en - throned a - bove all things;
So let my whole life be a blaz - ing of - fer - ing,

An - gels and saints cry out, we join them as we sing:
A life that shouts and sings the great - ness of our King.

*This song is included on the companion recording. Intro on recording is 8 measures.

Copyright © 2009 Thankyou Music (PRS) (adm. worldwide at EMICMGPublishing.com)
excluding Europe which is adm. by Kingswaysongs)/Worship Together Music (BMI)/
Sixsteps Bmi Designee (BMI) (adm. at EMICMGPublishing.com). All rights reserved. Used by permission.

He Lives

John 14:19; Rev. 1:18

73

A. H. A.

ALFRED H. ACKLEY

1. I serve a ris - en Sav - ior; He's in the world to - day. I know that He is liv - ing, what - ev - er men may say. I see His hand of mer - cy, I hear His voice of
2. In all the world a - round me, I see His lov - ing care; And though my heart grows wea - ry, I nev - er will de - spair. I know that He is lead - ing through all the storm - y
3. Re - joice, re - joice, O Chris - tian! lift up your voice and sing E - ter - nal hal - le - lu - jahs to Je - sus Christ, the King! The Hope of all who seek Him, the Help of all who

© 1933 Word Music, LLC. All rights reserved. Used by permission.

74

You, You Are God*

2 Cor. 5:14-15; Heb. 13:15

W. B.

WALKER BEACH

*This song is included on the companion recording. Intro on recording is 10 measures.

© 2003 Gateway Create Publishing (BMI)/Integrity's Praise Music (BMI)
(both adm. at EMICMGPublishing.com). All rights reserved. Used by permission.

I want my life to praise You.

I Have a Hope

75

Ps. 23:6; Jer. 29:11; Rom. 8:28, 31; 1 Cor. 2:9-10; Col. 1:27

T. W.

TOMMY WALKER

Unison (or opt. 2-part) Sing cues 2nd time

1. I have a hope, I have a fu-ture; I have a
(3. My God is) for me; He's not a-gainst me. So tell me

des-ti-ny that is yet a-wait-ing me. My life's not
whom then, tell me whom then shall I fear? He has pre-

o-ver, a new be-gin-ning's just be-gun; I have a
pared for me great works He'll help me to com-plete. I have a

Copyright © 2007 Doulos Music/BMI (admin. by Universal Music - Brentwood Benson Songs).
All rights reserved. Used by permission.

hope,   I have a hope.
hope,   I have a hope.

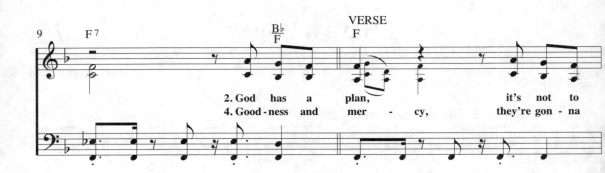

VERSE

2. God has a plan,   it's not to
4. Good-ness and mer - cy,   they're gon - na

harm me;   But it's to pros-per me   and to
fol - low me.   And I'll for - ev - er dwell   in the

hear me when I call. He in - ter - cedes for me,   work-in'
house of my great King. No eye has ev - er seen   all He's pre -

The Cleansing Wave

Zech. 13:1; Rev. 7:14

76

PHOEBE PALMER

ALLIE LAPOINTE

1. O now I see the crim-son wave, The foun-tain
(2. I rise to) walk in heav'n's own light A-bove the

deep and wide; Je-sus, my Lord, might-y to
world and sin, With heart made pure, and gar-ments

save, Points to His wound - ed side. The
white, And Christ en-throned with - in.

CHORUS

cleans-ing stream, I see, I see! I plunge and O it

Copyright © 2009 by PsalmSinger Music/BMI (admin. by Music Services). All rights reserved.

77 Because of Your Love*

Titus 3:3-7

B. B. and P. B.

BRENTON BROWN
and PAUL BALOCHE

As we come in-to Your pres - ence, we re-member ev - 'ry bless - ing that You've poured out so free-ly from a - bove. Lift-ing grat - i-tude and prais - es for com - pas - sion so a - maz-

*This song is included on the companion recording. Intro on recording is 8 measures.

Copyright © 2006 Thankyou Music (PRS) (adm. worldwide at EMICMGPublishing.com
excluding Europe which is adm. by Kingswaysongs)/Integrity's Hosanna! Music (ASCAP)
(adm. at EMICMGPublishing.com). All rights reserved. Used by permission.

You'll Come

78

Pss. 18:1-3; 27:14; Isa. 40:31; Mal. 4:2

BROOKE FRASER

1. I have de-cid - ed, I have re-solved to wait up - on You, Lord. My Rock and Re-deem - er, Shield and re - ward, I'll wait up - on You, Lord.

2. We are not shak - en, we are not moved, we wait up - on You, Lord. Might-y De-liv-er - er, our Tri - umph and Truth, we wait up - on You, Lord.

Copyright © 2007 Hillsong Publishing (APRA) (adm. in the US and Canada
at EMICMGPublishing.com) All rights reserved. Used by permission.

79 Victory in Jesus

Zech. 13:1; 1 Cor. 15:54-57

E. M. B.

EUGENE M. BARTLETT

Copyright 1939 by E.M Bartlett. Copyright renewed 1966 by Mrs. E.M. Bartlett.
Assigned to Albert E. Brumley & Sons/SESAC (admin. by ClearBox Rights).
All rights reserved. Used by permission.

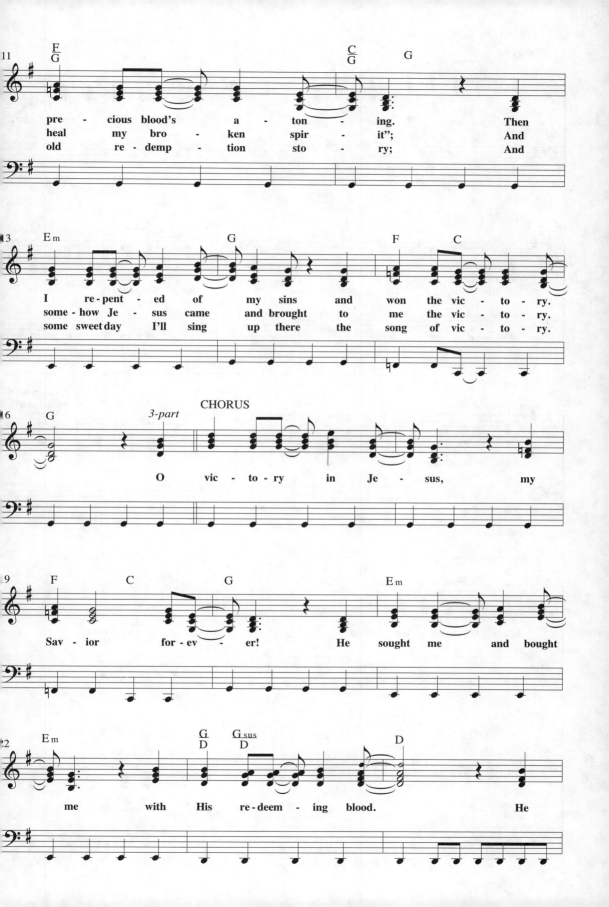

80

Rise and Sing*

Ps. 107:2; Isa. 52:7; 1 Cor. 15:20

S. F.

STEVE FEE

*This song is included on the companion recording. Intro on recording is 8 measures.

Copyright © 2009 Worship Together Music (BMI) Sixsteps Bmi Designee (BMI)
(adm. at EMICMGPublishing.com). All rights reserved. Used by permission.

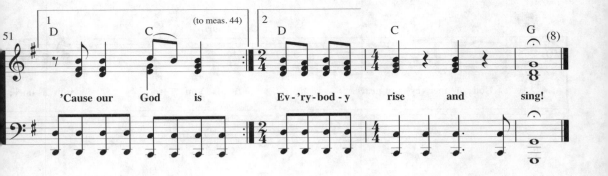

It Is You

Isa. 6:3; Matt. 18:20

81

PETER FURLER

'Cause our God is Ev-'ry-bod-y rise and sing!

As we lift up our hands will You meet us here?

As we call on Your name will You meet us here?

We have come to this place to wor-ship You,

Copyright © 2002 Ariose Music (ASCAP) (adm. at EMICMGPublishing.com).
All rights reserved. Used by permission.

They'll Know We Are Christians by Our Love

82

John 13:35

P. S.

PETER SCHOLTES

1. We are one in the Spir- it, we are one in the
(2. We will) walk with each oth- er, we will walk hand in

Lord. We are one in the Spir- it, we are one in the
hand. We will walk with each oth- er, we will walk hand in

Lord. And we pray that all u- ni- ty may one day be re-
hand. And to- geth- er we'll spread the news that God is in our

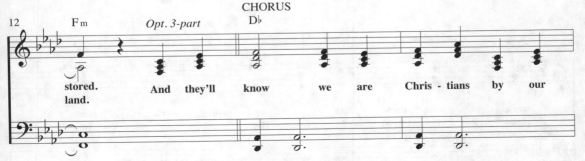

stored. And they'll know we are Chris- tians by our
land.

Copyright © 1966 F.E.L. Publications. Assigned 1991 Lorenz Publishing Company.
All rights reserved. Used by permission.

83 The Time Has Come

2 Cor. 5:14-15

J. H.

♩ = ca. 144

VERSE

JOEL HOUSTON

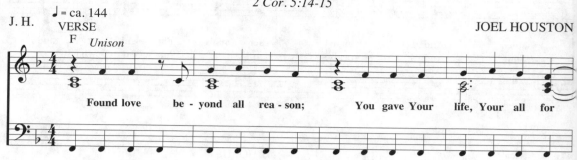

Found love be - yond all rea - son; You gave Your life, Your all for

me; And called me Yours for - ev - er.

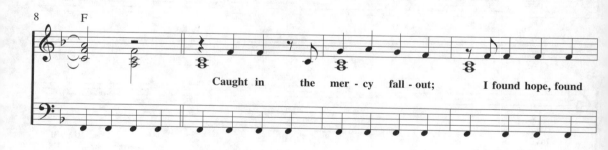

Caught in the mer - cy fall - out; I found hope, found

life, found all I need; You're all I need.

Copyright © 2004 Hillsong Publishing (APRA) (adm. in the US and Canada
at EMICMGPublishing.com) All rights reserved. Used by permission.

84 How Great Thou Art

Ps. 104:1-4; Rom. 8:32

S. K. H.

STUART K. HINE

1. O Lord, my God, when I in awe - some
2. When through the woods and for - est glades I
3. And when I think that God, His Son not
4. When Christ shall come with shout of ac - cla -

won - der Con - sid - er all the worlds Thy hands have
wan - der And hear the birds sing sweet - ly in the
spar - ing, Sent Him to die, I scarce can take it
ma - tion And take me home, what joys shall fill my

made, I see the stars, I hear the roll - ing
trees, When I look down from loft - y moun - tain
in; That on the cross, my bur - den glad - ly
heart! Then I shall bow in hum - ble ad - o -

Copyright © 1949 & 1953 The Stuart Hine Trust. All rights in the U.S.A. except print rights administered by EMI CMG.U.S.A. Print rights administered by Hope Publishing Company, Carol Stream, IL 60188. All rights reserved. Used by permission.

Thee. How great Thou art! How great Thou

Repeat ending (to meas. 1) | **Modulation ending**

art! 2. When through the art!
3. And when I
4. When Christ shall

♩ = ca. 80 **CHORUS**

Then sings my soul, my Sav - ior God, to

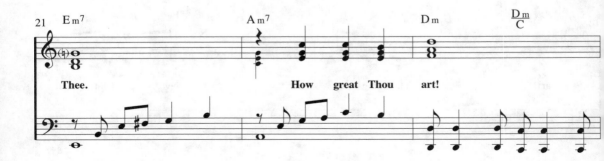

Thee. How great Thou art!

85

Face to Face

Gen. 32:30; Job 19:25-27; 1 Cor. 13:12

CARRIE BRECK and
ALLIE LAPOINTE

ALLIE LAPOINTE

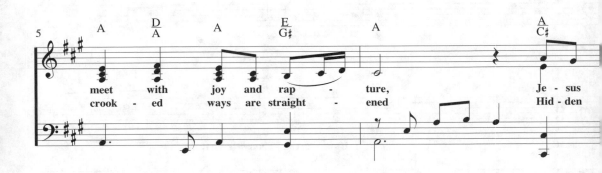

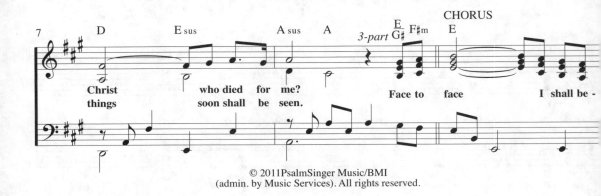

© 2011 PsalmSinger Music/BMI
(admin. by Music Services). All rights reserved.

Index of Scripture Backgrounds

*Songs marked with an asterisk (*)
are included on the companion recordings.

Index of Keys and Meter Signatures

*Songs marked with an asterisk (*)
are included on the companion recordings.*

Topical Index with Keys

*Songs marked with an asterisk (*) are included on the companion recordings.

INVITATION

JESUS CHRIST—LORDSHIP

JESUS CHRIST—RESURRECTION

JESUS CHRIST—SUFFERING, DEATH, & ATONEMENT

MAJESTY OF GOD

MISSIONS & EVANGELISM

PALM SUNDAY

PRAISE & CELEBRATION

Alphabetical Index with Keys

*Songs marked with an asterisk (*)
are included on the companion recordings.